I0481280

Free Reader Resources!

Just to say thanks for reading my book, I've included downloadable training assets I developed as part of my 3-step system.

I refer to these resources throughout the book, and rather than reinvent the wheel, you can download and use them right away, at no cost whatsoever.

- ✓ Big Deal Roadmap: 10-step infographic of the "Must Win" sales campaign process.
- ✓ Big Deal Relationship Map: helps you keep track of where you stand with key stakeholders you need to meet and influence.
- ✓ The Rapid Assessment Review: a one-page "Cheat Sheet" with all the qualification questions.
- ✓ Top 10 Inspection Tracker: helps you keep score—Won/Lost/Deferred/No Decision.

DOWNLOAD HERE:

SalesLeadersOnly.com/bookassets

*A Sales Leaders Guide to WIN More
Big Deals With My Proven 3-Step System*

WINNING
THE SIX-FIGURE
SALE

JEFF GOLDSTEIN

CONTENTS

FOREWORD

I hate missing my sales forecast. I don't know any serious sales leader who doesn't. You commit a number; you've got to hit it. Period. Full stop. Earlier in my career, it just seemed easier. I don't know if it's because the quota was smaller, the market was less crowded, or the competition wasn't as fierce, but it just seemed easier.

As my business grew, everything seemed to get more complicated, and winning big deals became much more difficult. The goal was bigger, and there was no way to get past the number without winning our unfair share of big deals. I can't tell you how many anxious Friday evenings I spent with my team trying to help get that one last deal across the finish line so we would make the quarter.

If you're a sales leader, you know what I mean!

Winning big deals is critical to your success. And so when Jeff asked me to write the Foreward to his new book, *Winning the Six-Figure Sale*, I just smiled.

I've known Jeff for the last 20 years. For 15 of those years, he was my boss at NetApp® Canada. (NetApp is a $5B Data Management company head-quartered in Silicon Valley.)

While Jeff was the VP and GM responsible for the Canadian subsidiary, I was the Western Canadian sales leader. I worked alongside Jeff and the rest of the Canadian leadership team to help scale the business. Together, we grew the Canadian operation from $17M with 15 people to over $200M and 125 people during the 15 years Jeff was VP. When Jeff left NetApp, he tagged me as the Canadian GM, and I've been running the business ever since.

Writing the Foreward for this book has been easy for me to do. I've worked with Jeff forever and have had a firsthand view of him developing and implementing the concepts he covers in this book.

Winning the Six-Figure Sale is all about helping sales teams win big deals—the deals that move the forecast needle. It's all about helping sales leaders inspect, assess and coach their teams to accelerate and yes..... win more *big deals*!

As Jeff says all the time, most sales leaders get promoted because they're great salespeople. They get anointed and handed a big sales target with virtually no sales leadership training. They have instinct and experience but no training or system to help their teams execute complex sales campaigns.

This book is a sales leader's guide to win more big deals using Jeff's 3-step system. It's his masterclass boiled down to a 90-minute read for sales leaders and their senior reps who have no time to read 400-page sales books.

I've lived Jeff's system for 15 years. In the early days, the process was informal and all about inspecting the quality of large sales campaigns Jeff called "Big Rock Reviews."

Jeff has taken the early concepts and built a 3-step system he now teaches to sales leaders all over North America. Jeff's system is all about helping sales leaders create a cadence to inspect the big deals in their sales funnels, assess the quality of their teams' sales campaigns early in the forecast process and then coach their teams to accelerate and win more big deals.

It's all about what to do after finding a big deal you need to ruthlessly qualify and then win.

This book will transform the way you think about helping your team run their complex sales campaigns. Rather than executing with a tactical one-step -at-a-time approach, leaders learn how to zoom out and see the entire chessboard. Teams become much more strategic and accelerate and WIN more big deals.

There is no ivory tower theory in this book. Jeff has inspected, assessed and coached sales teams through hundreds of sales campaigns using the approach he outlines in his book, so it's battle-tested and proven. He'll help you sharpen your skills, so you no longer rely solely on instinct and experience to be more successful.

Imagine the impact winning just one additional big deal per rep each quarter would have on your forecast accuracy, sales results, and income!

Enjoy the book and see if it isn't the best 90 minutes you've spent sharpening the saw to help you be a better sales leader, and yes, win more six-figure sales.

–Benny Cifelli
General Manager, NetApp Canada

WHO SHOULD READ
THIS BOOK?

I wrote this book for you if you're a sales leader who needs to win big deals to overachieve your sales targets.

- If you're a first-line sales manager running a sales district and looking for a better way to add value to your team's six– (and seven–) figure sales campaigns, this book's for you.
- If you're a second line sales director, with sales managers reporting to you and want to qualify if large sales opportunities will close when forecasted, this book's for you.
- If you're a sales VP, GM or country leader who owns the sales number and wants to checkpoint the progress of big deals in the forecast, then yes, this book's for you.

- And if you're a sales rep or single contributor who leads and collaborates with other team members to mount complex sales campaigns, this book is also for you.

Quick and Easy to Read

I've designed this book to be read in about 90 minutes because I know you're already way too busy. These days, sales leaders don't have the time or patience to spend hours reading a 400-page book looking to find those few nuggets of new gold.

But don't let its small size fool you. I've packed this book with my 3-step system's details that have enabled me to transform how sales leaders think about and manage the big deals in their sales pipelines.

While I'm an engineer by training, I've spent my entire career grinding out a sales number every week, month and quarter. I've carried a bag, led a sales district, region and country. I've always been close to the field, close to customers and partners, and close to the sales teams who make it all happen. So, I understand the life you've chosen as a sales leader and promise not to waste your time.

This Book Isn't Just for Tech Leaders

While my experience and the examples I use in the book are based on my 25 years leading the Canadian subsidiaries of large US-based technology companies, this book will help you even if you're not in tech. If your team runs complex sales campaigns that take months to close and involve multiple steps and stakeholders, this book will help you.

In Canada, I owned all the customer segments for the country. SMB (small deal size but lots of transactions), commercial (medium deal size), enterprise (large deal size), public sector (medium and large deals) and Cloud/SaaS (recurring revenue transactions).

This book will help you with every segment other than SMB. In smaller accounts, where sales reps can speak directly to a buyer who has a problem and the discretionary authority to spend their budget, this book will be overkill. But in every other segment where the Top 10 deals in your pipeline are large and complex, this book will help you.

Most Sales Leaders Have Instinct and Experience, But...

In my experience, most sales leaders have lots of processes and system training for managing their business, except for inspecting, assessing and coaching their teams to help accelerate and win their big deals. Sales leaders have experience and instinct but very little training or structured planning around big deal management.

This book will give you an intentional and deliberate process—a 3-step system—to transform the way you think about and help your team execute their "Must Win" sales campaigns.

What This Book Is and Is NOT About

Before I go into more detail about what you can expect from this book, let me take a moment and tell you what this book is not about.

This book is **NOT** about:

- Funnel building
- Appointment setting
- Objection handling
- Marketing
- Account planning

These are all essential sales activities but not what we're going to cover here. There are many excellent books and lots of sales training courses already out there full of information to help you at the top of your sales funnel.

This Book Is Different

This book is all about helping you dramatically improve your big deal forecast accuracy and win rates by helping your team execute better "Must Win" sales campaigns. This book is narrow in scope but very deep!

The 3-step system we cover in this book will help you:

- ✓ Develop an intentional and deliberate cadence to **INSPECT** your sales funnel and identify critical "Must Win" sales campaigns this quarter and next.
- ✓ Quickly **ASSESS** and ruthlessly qualify your team's sales campaigns early in the forecast process with a Rapid Assessment Review (15 minutes) called BANT.
- ✓ **COACH** your team by executing a Sales Strategy Review (45 minutes), so they never miss important steps or stakeholders that could crash their deals.

You'll also learn how to implement the 3-step system either on your own or with my help.

The 3-step system we cover in this book will help your team win more *big deals!*

INTRODUCTION

As I was researching this book, I was thinking about how I could test a little theory that had been kicking around in my head for the past several years. It had been bothering me a lot, and I was wondering if I was the only sales leader thinking about this problem.

And then it hit me. Rather than send another LinkedIn survey, why don't I go old school and pick up the phone and call 40 of my colleagues who run some of the largest, most successful tech companies in Canada? I knew most of them well, having spent my entire career leading the Canadian subsidiaries of several large US-based tech companies.

And so that's what I did. I took the time and personally called 40 of my colleagues and asked each leader these two simple questions.

1. What process or system do you use to make sure the big deals you're counting on in your forecast close when expected?

2. Other than the forecast call, how do you assess the quality of your team's sales campaigns so you don't get nasty surprises at the end of the quarter?

While each leader described what they did a little differently, they were all saying the same thing. Other than the forecast call, they had no intentional or deliberate process or system to review their big deals.

I Was Surprised!

They all complained that their forecasts were very inconsistent, yet most of them had no strategy to inspect the big deals that moved the forecast needle.

Most of the sales leaders told me that close to 50% of their quarterly sales funnel were made up of less than 10–20 big deals, yet 95% of them had no structured process or system to inspect, assess and coach their teams through the big deals in their funnels!

As most senior sales leaders will tell you, the entire forecasting process is a combination of art, science and fiction. Modern CRM systems tell the leader a lot about where the rep believes they are in the sales cycle but doesn't provide any insight into the sales campaign's quality.

I believe it's pure folly to depend on the weekly forecast call to drill down into complex sales campaigns in the very limited time you have to roll up a number. Yet that's what most all of the 40 leaders I spoke with told me was the primary way they determined which deals made it into the forecast.

Your Job Is to Make the News, Not Report It

My old boss at NetApp was Eric Mann, with whom I worked for 12 of my 15 years there. He ran the Americas for NetApp and owned a $2B sales number. He would always tell me that my job as VP of Canada was not to "report the news" (he could read the same reports that I did). My job was to go out and "make the news." The best way to do that was to actively engage with the sales teams driving big deals to help ensure they closed when expected.

All of the sales leaders I spoke with agreed that winning their large six– (and seven–) figure sales campaigns was the only way to beat their forecast consistently and grow their businesses.

This Book Is Not About Forecasting

Before you think this book is all about sales forecasting, I can assure you, it is not! But the only way to consistently beat your forecast is to win your unfair share of big deals.

Winning the Six-Figure Sale is all about leveraging the 3-step system that I have developed and refined during my tenure leading the Canadian subsidiaries at both NetApp and Veeam® Software, so you don't have to invent your own.

This Book Will Show You How to:

- ✓ Step 1: **Inspect** your sales funnel and develop a consistent cadence to review your top deals.
- ✓ Step 2: **Assess** and ruthlessly qualify the big deals early in the forecast process.
- ✓ Step 3: **Coach** your sales teams so they don't miss any steps or stakeholders that could sink their deals.
- ✓ Implement the 3-step system in your business.

Throughout the book, I'll include sales lessons I learned during difficult economic times. Whether they're broad economic downturns or industry-specific dips, my 3-step system will help you avoid the mistakes so many teams made during these disruptions.

At the end of each chapter, I'll include a short Chapter Summary to help make sure you catch every idea. I'll also include Action Items so you can begin to implement the chapter's ideas right away.

My hope is the practical, real-life examples I use will help you digest each chapter's content.

As my research confirmed, most sales leaders need a system other than the forecast call to *inspect, assess* and *coach* their teams but don't have time to invent a complete process of their own.

I hope that *Winning the Six-Figure Sale* gives you a new set of tools that take you way beyond gut instinct and experience to beat your competition and help your teams win more big deals—the deals that move the forecast needle.

Let's get started!

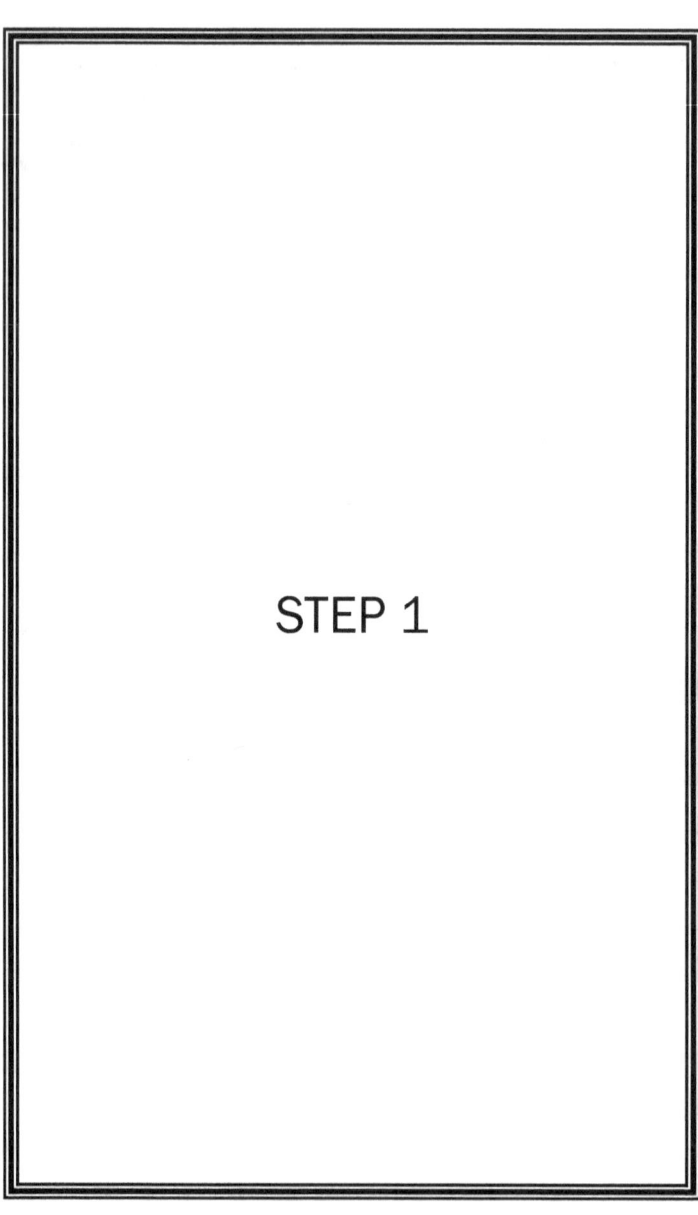

STEP 1

INSPECT THE SALES FUNNEL

CHAPTER 1

DO YOU HAVE A CADENCE TO INSPECT THE TOP 10 DEALS IN YOUR FUNNEL?

The first step of my 3-step system is funnel inspection. The whole purpose of this step is to take a much closer look at the big deals in your sales pipeline before you get surprised.

Here's a little exercise I use when teaching my program, Winning the Six-Figure Sale, to a group of sales leaders that always gets their attention. Imagine we're all together in a training room. I always start each class with the same question.

Do You Have a Specific Routine to Roll Up Your Weekly Forecast?

It doesn't matter if you run your forecast call in person or on the phone/Zoom, one-on-one or in a group. If you have a regular cadence to your forecast meeting, please stand up.

If I'm teaching a group of 20 sales leaders, 100% of the group stands up. No surprise, right? Everyone runs a regular forecast call. We're sales leaders, after all!

Then I ask the group:

Do you have a routine or cadence to review the Top 10 deals in your forecast? If you do, stay standing.

Most everyone stays standing until I challenge the group by saying the forecast call doesn't count. So, I ask the question again: Do you have a regular cadence to inspect the Top 10 deals in your forecast this quarter, OTHER than the forecast call? (As you'll see a bit later, the forecast call never has enough time to review complex sales campaigns thoroughly.)

Most of the leaders get a bit defensive, look around at their peers, and then 90% of them sit down.

Then I ask one last question:

Do you have a regular cadence to inspect the Top 10 deals in next quarter's sales funnel?

Most of the remaining sales leaders look at me like I have two heads, thinking who has time to pay attention to next quarter's big deals, and most everyone sits down. Maybe one or two out of twenty stays standing, but that's about it.

This Happens Every Time
I Do This Exercise...

99% of the group does regular forecasts calls, yet less than 5% of the group intentionally and deliberately inspect their Top 10–20 deals this quarter and next.

Before you get too lathered up, I'm not suggesting sales leaders don't spend time with their teams focused on big deals. They do. Sometimes on the phone, sometimes in the Starbucks coffee shop before visiting their prospect, and/or sometimes on their drive home from the office.

Sales leaders have been reviewing big deals using their instincts and experience forever, but not in a structured, repeatable way.

Imagine you're flying from Toronto to Montreal and have just settled into your seat. The silver-haired pilot enters the cockpit. He's been flying for twenty-five years and has flown this route a thousand times. The pilot looks over to his copilot and says to her, "I'm feeling good. The weather is clear to 10,000 feet. We're all fueled up, so tell the crew to shut the doors, and let's get this plane in the air."

That's Never Going to Happen, Ever!

Despite all the pilot's instinct and experience, both the pilot and copilot walk through a rigorous pre-flight routine, a checklist, before taking off to ensure they never miss important steps that could get them into trouble.

Now, remember the pilot is only doing one thing. He is flying the plane. He isn't replying to his kid's texts or emailing his wife to book their next vacation. He's laser-focused on this one task, and yet he uses a preflight checklist every single time he steps into the cockpit.

Now, the pilot has been trained this way, and this is simply how it's done in the aviation world to ensure everyone's safety.

So how is it that a highly trained pilot uses an intentional and deliberate process to do their job, yet sales leaders who coach multiple reps and do a hundred other things in a day have never been trained to inspect, assess and coach their team's big deals?

Yes, if a sales rep misses an important step or stakeholder, no souls are lost. But if you miss your number too many times, the consequences can be disastrous for both you and your family.

Most Sales Leaders
Were Great Sales Reps

Most sales leaders get promoted because they're great salespeople. They get anointed and handed a shiny new goal, and that's about the extent of their sales leadership and big deal training.

How much sales leadership training did you receive? How much of it was focused on what is perhaps the most critical component of hitting your number, closing your "Must Win" sales campaigns when expected?

Let me give you another example of why inspecting the big deals in your funnel with a specific cadence is so important.

In my last year leading Veeam Software's Canadian business, we had a new president, who set some very ambitious growth targets for the company.

The Canadian business needed to grow at 50% year over year, and at mid-year, we were only growing at 30%, so we were behind. I got a call from my boss, whom I knew very well, and his message was calm but clear.

"You're missing your forecast, and I need you to fix it fast. Worse yet, you start the quarter with great enthusiasm committing to hit the goal, and then each month, you take your forecast down and then finally miss the reduced number. Jeff, go figure this out!"

I knew he meant it.

In Canada, I owned all the customer segments for the country. The SMB business and Cloud recurring revenue business were both on track, so I knew my problem wasn't there. I suspected it was the bigger deals that were the issue.

The Devil Is in the Detail

So I got my operations manager, and we dug into the funnel data from the previous quarter. Here's what we did.

Step 1. We imported the 20 biggest deals from last quarter's sales funnel into Excel.

Quarterly - Big Deal Pipeline								
Sales Team	Sales Rep	Reseller	Account	Amount	WON	LOST	DEFERRED	NO DECISION
West	Stewart	Reseller 1	Account 1	$450,000.00	$450,000			
East	Bill	Reseller 1	Account 2	$475,000.00			$375,000	
West	Bob	Reseller 2	Account 3	$350,000.00			$350,000	
Central	John	Reseller 3	Account 4	$250,000.00			$250,000	
Central	Aaron	Reseller 4	Account 5	$240,000.00				$240,000
Central	John	Reseller 5	Account 6	$240,000.00			$240,000	
Central	John	Reseller 6	Account 7	$239,627.70				$239,628
West	Marshall	Reseller 7	Account 8	$216,000.00		$216,000		
West	Bill	Reseller 8	Account 9	$200,000.00				$200,000
West	Bill	Reseller 9	Account 10	$186,000.00			$186,000	
East	Steve	Reseller 10	Account 11	$150,000.00			$150,000	
East	Patrick	Reseller 1	Account 12	$107,351.71			$107,352	
West	Russ	Reseller 2	Account 13	$105,000.00	$105,000			
West	Stewart	Reseller 3	Account 14	$101,400.00			$101,400	
East	Patrick	Reseller 4	Account 15	$100,000.00				$100,000
East	All	Reseller 5	Account 16	$98,000.00	$98,000			
Central	Chris	Reseller 6	Account 17	$88,776.00			$88,776	
Central	Paul	Reseller 7	Account 18	$78,000.00	$78,000			
Central	Patrick	Reseller 8	Account 19	$79,000.00	$79,000			
Central	Eric	Reseller 9	Account 20	$75,900.00				$75,900
		Big Deal Pipe at start of Q1		$ 3,971,055	$ 999,000	$ 216,000	$ 1,848,528	$ 855,528
					25%	5%	45%	25%
		Total Pipeline at start of Q1		$ 8,000,000				
				50%				

Diagram 1—Big Deal Pipeline

Step 2. We then compared the total revenue of these 20 deals ($3.97m) against the entire funnel's total revenue from the last quarter ($8M). The top 20 deals represent 50% of the entire sales funnel. Yes, 50% from just 20 deals—I was shocked.

Step 3. I then went back into Salesforce® and tracked those 20 deals to see if the data would explain why we were missing our forecast.

At first, the data wasn't too surprising. The team had won five of their top 20 deals and lost only one. A 5:1 win/loss ratio was pretty good.

I kept digging and discovered that 9 of the top 20 deals (45%) got deferred into the next quarter. They didn't close when forecasted but weren't lost.

The final 5 top deals in the funnel simply disappeared.

- 5 deals (25%) were won in the current quarter.
- 1 deal (5%) was lost.
- 9 deals (45%) got deferred to next quarter.
- 5 deals (25%) disappeared with no decision.

THE BIG PROBLEM

Diagram 2—Won/Lost/Deferred/No Decision Tracker

The data freaked me out. Of all the top 20 deals in the forecast at the start of the quarter, 70% (deferred + no decision) did NOT close when expected, and we missed our forecast.

While everyone pays attention to wins and losses, no one keeps track of the deals that get deferred because we don't treat them as losses. But if you add the deals with no decision to the loss pile, the data tells an entirely different story.

Now the data shows we won five deals (25%), lost six deals (30%), and 45% of the remaining deals slipped to the next quarter.

Since the top 20 deals represented 50% of the total pipeline, having 70% of the top deals not closing made hitting the forecast impossible. And a good percentage of the deals that slipped were still in the forecast at the start of the third month.

Happy Ears and Nasty Surprises

The reps had happy ears on, and since they didn't have enough pipeline to backfill these poorly qualified deals, we lived in hope up until the end of the quarter when invariably, there were a bunch of very nasty surprises.

Does any of this sound familiar?

Do you get nasty forecast surprises at the end of the quarter, when deals the team has been calling all quarter long fall out of the forecast at the last minute?

- Do your reps have happy ears on?
- Is your team running quality sales campaigns?
- Are they selling wide and deep enough to win?

If you want to reduce last-minute forecast surprises, what can you do right now?

Step 1 of the System—
Implement a Big Deal Inspection Cadence

A big deal inspection cadence is the first step of my 3-step system and is easier than you might think to implement but does take discipline.

This first step is critical because it helps you identify the big deals you'll review in more detail in Steps 2 and 3 of the system, which I'll cover in upcoming chapters.

Here's how to get started with Step 1.

- Download the Big Deal Inspection Tracker in Diagram 3 from the resource page at SalesLeadersOnly.com/bookassets.
- Populate the data from your CRM system for your Top 10 deals this quarter.
- Populate the data from your CRM system for your Top 10 deals next quarter.

				Current Quarter				
Sales Rep	Deal Name	Assessment Review Date	Sales Strategy Review Date	$$ Value	WON	LOST	DEFERRED	NO DECISION
Rep Name	Deal 1	Date	Date	$357,000	$357,000			
Rep Name	Deal 2	Date	Date	$310,340	$310,340			
Rep Name	Deal 3	Date	Date	$268,430			$268,430	
Rep Name	Deal 4	Date	Date	$250,000		$250,000		
Rep Name	Deal 5	Date	Date	$225,000			$225,000	
Rep Name	Deal 6	Date	Date	$225,000				$225,000
Rep Name	Deal 7	Date	Date	$215,000				$215,000
Rep Name	Deal 8	Date	Date	$120,000	$120,000			
Rep Name	Deal 9	Date	Date	$115,000	$115,000			
Rep Name	Deal 10	Date	Date	$105,000	$105,000			$105,000
		Total ---------------->		$2,190,770	$1,007,340	$250,000	$ 803,430	$ 545,000
					46%	11%	37%	25%

				Next Quarter				
Sales Rep	Deal Name	Assessment Review Date	Sales Strategy Review Date	$$ Value	WON	LOST	DEFERRED	NO DECISION
Rep Name	Deal 1	Date	Date	$630,000				
Rep Name	Deal 2	Date	Date	$575,000				
Rep Name	Deal 3	Date	Date	$550,000				
Rep Name	Deal 4	Date	Date	$482,000				
Rep Name	Deal 5	Date	Date	$425,000				
Rep Name	Deal 6	Date	Date	$350,000				
Rep Name	Deal 7	Date	Date	$240,000				
Rep Name	Deal 8	Date	Date	$259,628				
Rep Name	Deal 9	Date	Date	$216,000				
Rep Name	Deal 10	Date	Date	$200,000				
		Total ---------------->		$3,907,628	$ -	$ -	$ -	$ -
					0%	0%	0%	0%

Diagram 3—Big Deal Inspection

Look Over the Horizon

I want to pause here and make a critical point. Most sales leaders make the mistake of only focusing on deals in the current quarter. Take the time to identify the big deals brewing next quarter and get them on your radar screen right now!

Your big deals take multiple quarters to close. You need to begin inspecting them months out if you want to impact the quality of your team's sales campaigns. Waiting until four weeks left to go in the quarter to inspect your big deals is way too late to impact their success.

The final step of your inspection process is to keep track of your Won, Lost, Deferred and No Decision categories as you progress through the quarter. Record the outcomes of your deals in the Inspection Tracker spreadsheet (diagram 3).

Gain New Perspective on Your Big Deals

At the end of the quarter, see if the data doesn't surprise you and give you new insights into what is happening with your big deals. After a few quarters, you'll have a whole new perspective on how well each sales rep on your team is executing against their forecasted big deals.

As you begin a new quarter, repeat the process.

You see, the inspection process is not that difficult, yet most sales leaders don't have the discipline to implement it. Will you be different?

Now you might be thinking, "Jeff, who has time for all this? I'm already running as fast as I can." In my opinion, this is not a time issue. It's a priority issue.

Let Me Explain

The average sales leader spends 40 hours a week at work. That's 160 hours a month at minimum.

In the coming chapters, I'll show you how to run a Big Rock Review, including the Rapid Assessment Review and the Sales Strategy Review, in less than one hour, no matter how complex the deal is.

So that's 20 hours (20 deals x 1 hour each), plus some prep time and follow-up. If you spend 30 hours inspecting, assessing and coaching your teams' big deals during the first two months of the quarter, that's less than 10% of your time focused on the big deals that drive your business.

In what other parts of your business can you spend 10% of your time and get such a significant return? Now imagine what would happen if you found even more time to spend on the big deals that moved your business!

In chapter #5, we'll talk about what you're going to have to stop doing to make time for the entire Big Rock Review process. You'll have some choices to make.

If your goal is to get more engaged with your sales teams and add value around their top sales campaigns, Big Deal Inspection becomes a critical *must - have*, not *would-like* leadership activity!

In the next chapter, I'll give you a quick overview of the Big Deal Roadmap. Think of it as a checklist of all the steps and stakeholders your team needs to meet and influence in a complex sales campaign. The roadmap will lay the foundation for what's to come.

In chapter #3, we'll discuss Step 2 of my system, where I'll show you how to run a "Rapid Assessment Review" to quickly assess the quality of your team's sales campaigns and help ensure your big deals are ruthlessly qualified.

In chapter #4, we'll cover Step 3 of my system, where I'll show you how to run a "Sales Strategy Review" to help coach your team through the remaining steps on the Big Deal Roadmap and ensure they cover all their bases.

And then, in chapter #5, we'll talk about how to implement the system in your business, either on your own or with my help.

Chapter Summary

I know you're busy, and there are many things to distract you even as you read this book. To help make sure you didn't miss anything, here is the first quick summary and action item list that I promised in the Introduction.

- The 3 steps in my system are INSPECT, ASSESS and COACH to help your team accelerate and win more big deals.

- 99% of all sales leaders do regular forecasts calls, yet less than 5% have an intentional and deliberate process to critically inspect their Top 10-20 deals in the current quarter.
- Most sales leaders don't inspect next quarter's big deals until it's way too late.
- Sales leaders have been reviewing big deals using their instincts and experience forever but not in a structured, repeatable way.
- Most sales leaders get promoted because they're great salespeople, not because they have training and systems in place to inspect, assess and coach their teams' big deals.

Action Items

Get started building your Big Deal Inspection cadence. Complete the following steps during the very first week of a new quarter.

- Download the Big Deal Inspection Tracker in Diagram 3 from the resource page at SalesLeadersOnly.com/bookassets.
- Populate the data from your CRM system for your Top 10 deals this quarter.

- Populate the data from your CRM system for your Top 10 deals next quarter.
- Keep track of Won, Lost, Deferred and No Decision.
- Review the data at the end of each quarter, and see what pops out at you!

We'll use the Inspection Tracker again in chapters #3 and #4, where we'll organize Rapid Assessment and Sales Strategy Reviews to dig into your team's sales campaigns.

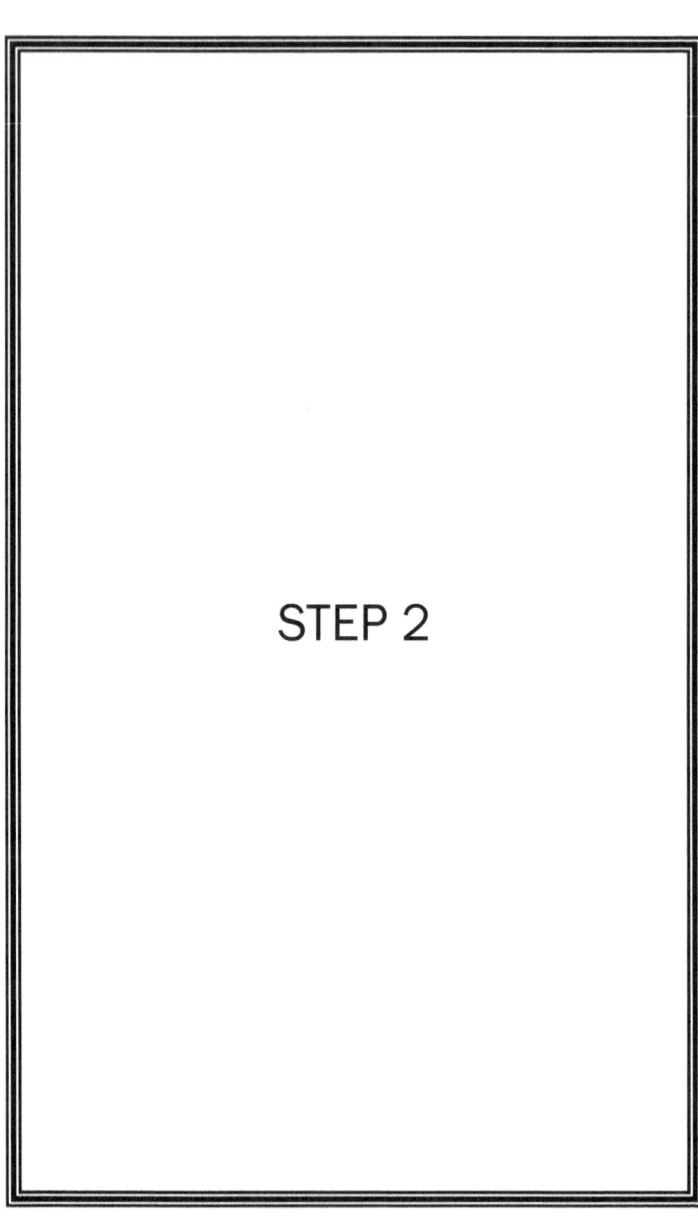

STEP 2

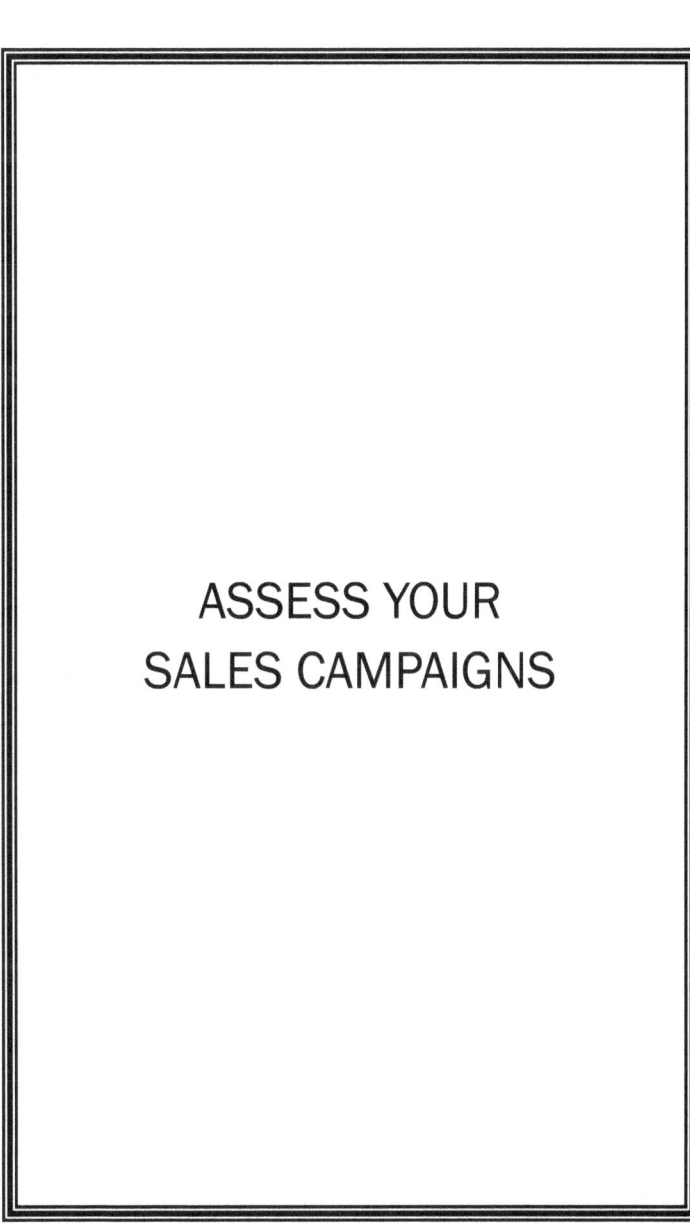

ASSESS YOUR
SALES CAMPAIGNS

CHAPTER 2

THE BIG DEAL ROADMAP

This chapter will lay the foundation for the next steps in my 3-step system. Since I know you want to get on with it, this chapter will be a high-level (quick) overview of the Big Deal Roadmap before we get to Steps 2 and 3 of the system.

Diagram 4 is an infographic I developed to help sales leaders zoom out and see the entire chessboard. You can download the Big Deal Roadmap from the book resource page at

SalesLeadersOnly.com/bookassets

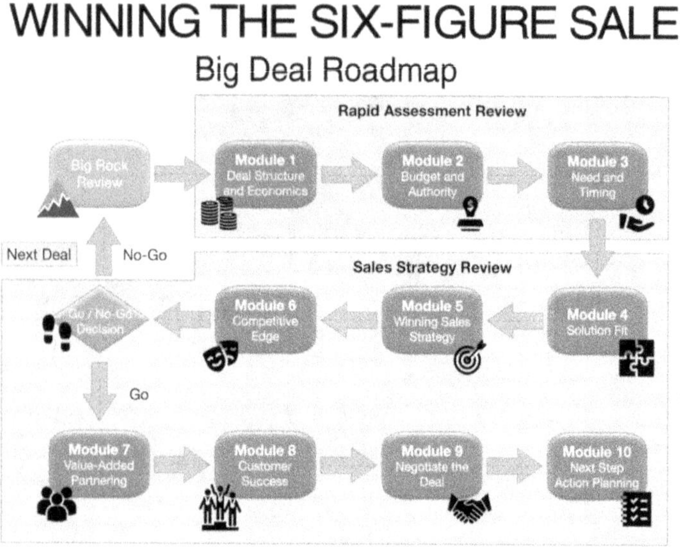

WINNING THE SIX-FIGURE SALE
Big Deal Roadmap

Rapid Assessment Review

Big Rock Review → Module 1 Deal Structure and Economics → Module 2 Budget and Authority → Module 3 Need and Timing

Next Deal | No-Go

Sales Strategy Review

Go / No-Go Decision ← Module 6 Competitive Edge ← Module 5 Winning Sales Strategy ← Module 4 Solution Fit

Go

Module 7 Value-Added Partnering → Module 8 Customer Success → Module 9 Negotiate the Deal → Module 10 Next Step Action Planning

Diagram 4—Big Deal Roadmap

The Roadmap Is My Version of the Preflight Routine or Checklist

In my, **Winning the Six-Figure Sale** half-day course, I go through each module of the roadmap in detail to help teach sales leaders how to assess and coach their teams to uncover and then address gaps in their sales campaigns.

But let's start with a brief overview of the roadmap and then cover the Rapid Assessment and Sales Strategy Reviews in chapters #3 and #4.

Affectionately, I call the entire preflight routine the "Big Rock Review." Big deals, big rocks, you get it!

Let's Start With the Overview

Module 1—Deal Structure and Economics

This is where the sales team outlines their "Single Sales Opportunity." What are they trying to sell and to whom?

Now, remember, this is not an account plan.

This is an opportunity/deal review where you have already identified a big deal you want to win. In this module, the team describes what they're selling in broad terms, including the deal size and expected future revenue opportunity if they win the deal. The team won't have a final configuration at this point but should understand their deal's broad strokes.

Module 2—Budget and Authority

In this module, the sales team describes what they know about their prospect's budget approval process.

I also introduce the Relationship Map, which is a much more effective way to describe who's in the prospect's powerbase than any organization chart could provide.

Module 3—Need and Timing

In addition to customer needs, we explore the business outcomes the proposed solution will provide.

Focusing on business outcomes is a differentiator we explore in more detail in the next chapter. We also cover three critical criteria that need to be addressed to ensure the solution gets funding.

Finally, we discuss the timing of your deal as well as the compelling event that will ensure your deal closes when forecasted.

Module 4—Solution Fit

This module explores what we know about the customer's selection criteria and reviews the execution plan to help the customer discover our value.

Module 5—Winning Sales Strategy

In this module, we explore sales strategies other than low price!

We discuss upgrades, land and expand, big bang replacement, new workloads, etc., as well as traps and land mines used to trip up your competitors.

We also discuss the competition's strategy to beat you.

Module 6—Competitive Edge

This is a module on the roadmap many sales leaders miss.

How do you build a competitive edge into your deal that gives you an advantage other than your product's features?

Developing an edge needs special attention and focus and takes time to develop, so it needs to be considered early in the campaign.

At this point in the review, I often pause and ask the team if they're ready to make a Go/No-Go decision.

Have we learned enough to validate that we have a good shot at winning the deal? Or are we best to bail now, before we waste any more cycles on a deal that's stacked against us?

Module 7—Value-Added Partnering

This is another module that many sales leaders miss, even though some companies do all their business through value-added Resellers.

This module aims to figure out how to create a force multiplier by partnering to bring more expertise to the customer. This step requires both parties to build trust in each other that becomes apparent to the customer.

When the vendor and partner work together, it's a beautiful thing.

When both parties don't pull their weight, things can get ugly in a hurry. In this module, I cover a few activities that both sales teams can do to dramatically improve how they communicate and work together that often gets overlooked.

Module 8—Customer Success

Again, this module often gets missed.

In this portion of the review, I always ask what the strategy is to ensure customer success before taking the customer's purchase order?

Does the sales team understand the risks that could cause the project to fail?

Most sales teams worry about customer success after the deal and often after the project gets off to a rocky start.

Module 9—Negotiating the Deal

This module seems obvious, but it's not.

I ask the sales team a few questions to see if they've thought through this final stage of their sales campaign.

If this is a new prospect they haven't done business with before, the answers aren't obvious or straightforward after all.

Module 10—Next Step Action Planning

In this final module, I ask the sales rep, whom I view as the quarterback of the deal, how they will keep track of all the action items they uncover in the review sessions?

And since the rep is not running the deal all by themself, I ask how they will hold their team accountable to get things done on time?

And then my last question is my favorite. You'll learn more about the "Look Back Question" in the next chapter.

Ok, There You Have It

Ten modules or steps in a complex sales campaign, and as you can see, there are a lot of moving parts.

Chapter Summary

Here's a quick summary and action items to help make sure you caught everything we covered.

Here are the Top 10 modules in a complex sales campaign. Use the Big Deal Roadmap as the preflight routine or checklist to cover all the bases.

- Module 1—Deal Structure and Economics
- Module 2—Budget and Authority
- Module 3—Need and Timing
- Module 4—Solution Fit
- Module 5—Winning Sales Strategy
- Module 6—Competitive Edge
- Module 7—Value-Added Partnering
- Module 8—Customer Success

- Module 9—Negotiating the Deal
- Module 10—Next Step Action Planning

Action Items

Download the Big Deal Roadmap infographic in Diagram 4 from the resource page at

SalesLeadersOnly.com/bookassets

CHAPTER 3

DO YOU HAVE A PROCESS TO ASSESS THE QUALITY OF YOUR SALES CAMPAIGNS?

A s you read in the last chapter, there are a lot of moving parts in a complex sales campaign.

So how do you assess the quality of your team's top sales campaigns early in the forecast process? The last thing you want as a sales leader is to include big deals in your forecast with no chance of closing in the current quarter.

But how can you tell without getting under the hood and taking a closer look?

That's what the Big Rock Review is all about. It's a structured approach and includes questions to ask your sales team as you walk through the big deal roadmap. These questions give you a repeatable process to ensure the team doesn't miss important steps or stakeholders that could sink their deal.

But rather than book an hour and do the entire review in one meeting, I've found it far more effective to tackle the review in two steps.

Quick Overview of the Process

The first step is to schedule a Rapid Assessment Review (15 minutes) for all deals on the Big Deal Inspection Tracker (from chapter #1). Include deals from the current quarter as well as next.

These reviews should include the sales leader and rep only.

Once you've completed the **Rapid Assessment Review** and determined the deal is real and well - qualified, then organize a second 45-minute meeting, which we call the Sales Strategy Review.

At this meeting, include the broader sales team, which includes the sales rep, their technical presale resources and anyone else directly involved in the deal.

In the **Sales Strategy Review**, you go deeper into the campaign's sales strategy and ask more in-depth questions to challenge the team and help them identify gaps in their campaign that need to be addressed.

Once you implement my 3-step system, you're going to see a lot of big deals (10–20 each quarter). You'll get good at connecting dots, pointing your reps in the right direction, and sharing the best practices you've seen from other deals in your business.

You'll also learn to spot BS quickly and call it out so you can get the team focused back on reality.

As the leader, it will be your job to keep the reviews crisp and laser-focused. By working through the review one question at a time in the correct order, I've found that you can keep everyone on task so the reviews don't take longer than they need to.

Step 2 of the System—
The Rapid Assessment Review

Let's get into Step 2 of the system, and I'll show you how to run a Rapid Assessment Review right now.

Download the Rapid Assessment Review "Cheat Sheet" from the book assets page. It includes all the questions we're going to cover. Print it and follow along.

The whole goal of this step in the process is to get a good feel for how qualified the deal is, especially if the rep is planning to or has already included the deal in this quarter's forecast.

Get the Reviews Scheduled

Before you can do a review, it needs to be scheduled. This is one of the most critical steps in the entire process. At NetApp, I had an admin who took care of all the scheduling. At Veeam, I did not.

I can tell you that getting all the reviews into the calendar can take some effort and perseverance. Your reps will be a bit uncertain about the whole process initially, and you'll hear some creative excuses for why the date you proposed doesn't work.

Keep at it. Help your reps understand this is not voluntary, and since you're the boss, this is one of the times you just need to be, well, the boss.

It gets easier as your reps go through a few reviews and discover their value. Get all the calendaring work done during the first week of the quarter, so everyone knows when their review is to be completed.

Here Are the Questions to Ask in the Review

Module 1—Deal Structure and Economics

The first questions I ask are about the structure of the deal and its economics.

If it's a big deal, it might have significant discounts, which could impact the deal's profit margins. In many organizations, these aggressive deals need approval beyond the first-line sales leader and often go through a formal deal desk approval process.

This first module includes a basic description of the rep's deal or "Single Sales Opportunity."

- What is the rep selling?
- How big is the deal?
- What discounts or gross margin levels do you expect to have to sell at?
- When is the deal forecasted to close?
- Who needs to approve this deal?

You don't need to see final configurations at this point but merely the broad strokes of what the rep is proposing.

If the team already has a final configuration or a firm and final price, you're doing the Rapid Assessment Review way too late in the process. With a few weeks left in the quarter, there is not much you can do to change the deal's direction. It's simply too late, so complete the review early in the sales process. This is easy to do if you're already reviewing next quarter's deals.

To help give me more context about the deal, I always ask:

- What additional revenue can we expect over the next 12–24 months if we win the deal?

Sometimes we need to be very aggressive to land the first sale (even if it's small) because there's a lot of annuity revenue behind this first transaction.

Sometimes it's a big one-shot deal with no annuity business for the next three years (we still like those). It's essential to understand the difference.

If this is an annuity deal with future revenue, I always ask the team:

- What is the "get-well" plan so we don't have to sell the future annuity business at these same aggressive discount/gross margin levels?

It may be ok to be very aggressive to win the deal, but having a plan to structure the future business so you can reduce discounts and improve profit margins is what I call the "get-well" plan.

We cover this in more detail in the Sales Strategy Review in the next chapter, but I like to get the rep thinking about their overall sales strategy early in their sales campaign.

And the final question I ask in this section is:

- Are there likely to be any special Terms and Conditions which could be challenging for the legal team to accept?

This early in the sales campaign, and long before the negotiations have begun, it might be difficult to tell. If the rep is selling to a Fortune 500 company, big bank or large government entity, there may be terms like Most Favored Nation (MFN) or Liability and Indemnity that will need to be considered.

These are not terms that can be negotiated in the last few days of the quarter, so you want to flush these types of terms out as early as possible so your company has time to deal with them.

Module 2—Qualifying Budget and Authority

To make qualifying the deal simple, remember the acronym, BANT; I think IBM was the first to use this methodology ages ago, so I've tuned it up to make the questions even more relevant today.

Think BANT:

- ✓ B = Budget
- ✓ A = Authority
- ✓ N = Need/Business Outcomes
- ✓ T = Timing

Let's tackle the Budget and Authority first with a few more questions.

<u>B = Budget</u>

- Has the budget been approved?
- More importantly, has the budget been released and now available to be spent?
- What's changed in the customers' approval process?

When the economy slows down, sales reps need to pay special attention and ask what's changed in the customers' approval process. If the answer is nothing, that's a huge red flag.

In previous slowdowns, managers' signing authority was reduced, often without the managers' knowledge. Deals required extra scrutiny before purchase orders were released, even if the funds had already been budgeted.

These additional steps and signatures take extra time and often cause quarter-end deadlines to be missed, creating big surprises for both the rep and sales leader!

A = Authority

- Is the rep speaking with the decision maker who has discretionary ability to spend the budget?
- Have they met them in person?

Real Authority Is Critical

Is the rep speaking to the person who owns the budget? Or are they merely talking to someone who executes on a budget held by someone else? There's a big difference. Does the person they're speaking with have the authority to prioritize the budget even when it is reduced?

Unless the rep has sold the value of the solution to the budget owner, they are relying on someone else (often a technical recommender) to defend the budget during budget cut meetings.

It's not likely to happen and a big reason why projects get deferred!

Personal meetings may be hard to get, but looking the decision maker in the eye to confirm that they are planning to move forward is way better than emailing or text messaging. And if the decision maker will agree to meet with you, that's a great buy signal.

If the Decision Maker Won't Agree to Meet, That's Generally Not A Good Thing

I developed a straightforward tool I call the Relationship Map that is far more effective at helping figure out who's in the customer's power base than a traditional org chart (Diagram 5, download it on the resource page and follow along).

It's a simple diagram created in Excel that I get the rep to complete before the review. In each upper-level box, the rep identifies the decision maker's name, role and title. Below that are three additional boxes they complete.

- In Box 1: Have you met the decision maker in person? Y or N
- In Box 2: Is the decision maker pro (+), neutral (=), gainst (-), Mentor (M), Unknown (UKN)?
- In Box 3: Is the person in the power base a decision maker (D), direct influencer (DI), indirect influencer (II), unknown (UKN)?

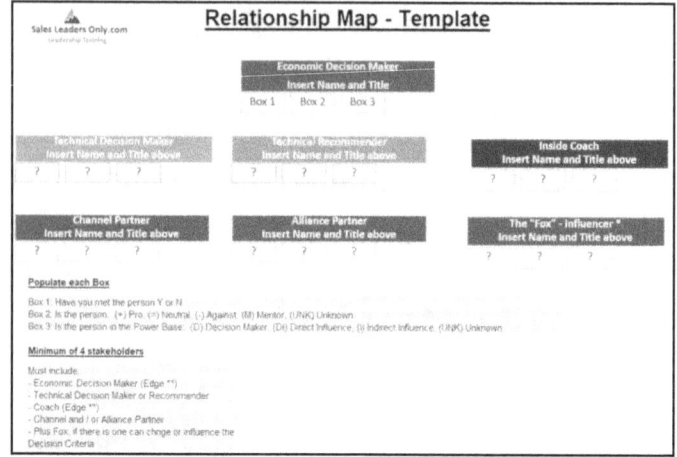

Diagram 5—Relationship Map

This is one of the most important diagrams in the entire review process and should be shared with the full account team. You can tell a tremendous amount about how wide and deep the team is selling from this one simple diagram that takes the rep 5 minutes to complete if they're running a complete campaign and know their stuff.

Reviewing the Relationship Map helps me understand if the team is running both technical and financial/political campaigns.

If the team has only focused on the technical recommender and technical decision makers, they won't know much about essential decision makers in the other boxes.

Many sales teams, especially in technology, think it's all about their solution's technical capabilities and focus all of their energy on the technical relationships inside the account.

Without a solid plan to follow the money (meet the financial decision maker) and understand the decision-making process's politics, the deal is at risk.

The Harvard Business Review (Diagram 6) did a study several years ago and concluded that the average buying group in a complex sale included 5.4 decision makers. That number is closer to 6.5 today.

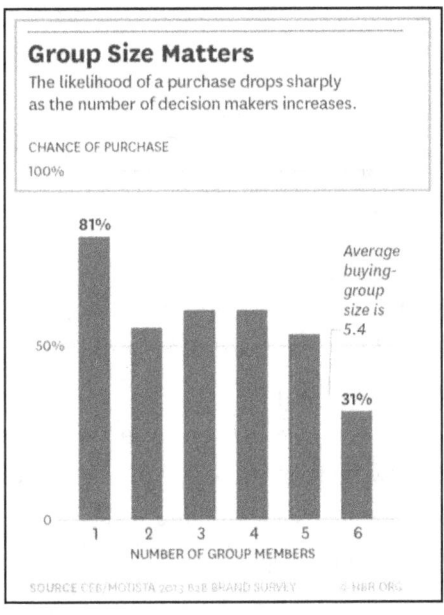

Diagram 6—Buying Group Size

As the number of decision makers increases, the likelihood of a deal happening decreases significantly.

Do you think there are more or less decision makers involved in determining if money should be spent on a project in difficult economic times? Happy ears off, I think you know the answer!

Sales teams need access to power to truly qualify if money will be spent on a specific project. In tough economic times, it's generally a VP level title (VP of finance, VP of I.T. etc.), not a technical manager or director who has the discretionary ability to get funds released and spent on six– and seven–figure deals.

If you're not selling to power, your project is at risk! To be successful, the team needs to be selling wide and deep and covering ALL their bases, both technical and financial.

Module 3—Needs and Timing
<u>N = Need/Business Outcomes</u>

What type of projects are highly likely to get funding? At the VP level, it's all about business outcomes, not technical capabilities.

Ask yourself these three questions, and think about the answers from your customers' perspective.

- Is the project strategically relevant?
- Is the project tactically urgent?
- Does the project provide rapid time-to-value?

Projects must meet all three of the following criteria to get approved in difficult economic times: 1.) strategically relevant, 2.) tactically urgent, and 3.) provide a rapid time-to-value ratio. Deals that don't meet these criteria may still get approved but will likely take longer to close, once again causing you to miss your forecast.

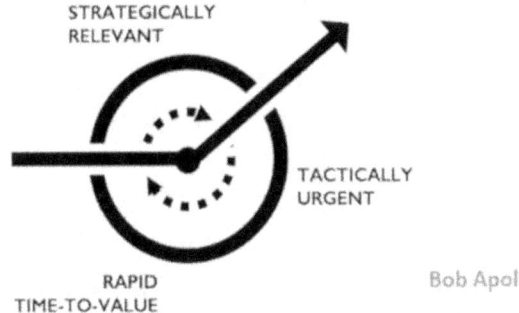

Diagram 7—Project Approval Criteria

I was chatting with the VP of sales of one of Canada's largest technology distributors back in June of 2020 (right in the middle of the first COVID-19 wave) and asked him how his business was doing. He said, "Jeff, if we had another 15,000 laptops in stock, we would have sold them."

Work from home capabilities became strategically relevant, tactically urgent and provided rapid time–to–value.

Sales reps working on 3-year business process re-engineering projects were having a much tougher time getting their projects to move forward.

T = Timing

The final area I explore in the Rapid Assessment Review is the timing of the deal.

The first question I ask is:

- What is the compelling event that will ensure the deal closes when forecasted?

Reps often struggle with this question and say things like their pricing is time-stamped and only valid for this quarter or their maintenance agreement expires at the end of the month.

Customers are way too smart these days for these tactics to work. Customers expect the price you offered on Friday will be the same price they pay on Monday, even if it's after your quarter-end.

There is way too much competition in the marketplace today to make time-stamped pricing concessions a real compelling event. Sorry, they just aren't!

The next question I ask is even more critical.:

- What happens if the customer misses the compelling event?

If nothing happens, from the customer's perspective, it's simply not a compelling event that would ensure the deal closes when expected.

Other important questions are:

- Can the rep clearly articulate WHY the customer needs to make the purchase now?
- What is the negative outcome if they do not make the purchase?

As an example: If the customer has built out a new data center and can't meet their go-live date without your equipment, that's pretty compelling, especially if they have already bought other equipment to meet their deadline.

Not every deal has a compelling event, but without one, sales cycles tend to take longer than expected, sometimes much longer, further reducing the accuracy of your forecast.

Whether you sell hardware, software, cloud/SaaS services or industrial equipment, large customer procurements take longer to get approved as more steps and decision makers get added to the approval/procurement process.

And while sales reps everywhere are under tremendous pressure to get their deals across the finish line, no amount of pressure or quarter-end incentives will get deals out of the oven before they're done.

There are just too many eyes on big deals to make them happen until the customer (not the vendor) is ready!

If the rep has covered their bases using the BANT methodology, this first step in the Big Rock Review shouldn't take much longer than 15 minutes.

- The **B**udget has been approved and released.
- The rep is speaking with the buyer, who has discretionary **A**uthority to spend the budget.
- The **N**eeds and business outcomes are strategically relevant, tactically urgent and provide rapid time–to– value.
- There is a compelling event that will trigger the sale to close on **T**ime.

That Wraps up the Rapid Assessment Review

Now that the project has been ruthlessly qualified, let's go on to the next chapter and the Sales Strategy Review.

Chapter Review

Here's a quick summary and action items to help make sure you caught everything we covered.

- During the first week of the quarter, get all the Rapid Assessment Reviews for this quarter and next into the calendar. Don't take any excuses from the reps!

- The Big Rock Review's first step is a 15-minute Rapid Assessment Review.
- Module 1 is a quick review of the project's structure and economics:
  - ✓ What is the rep selling?
  - ✓ How big is the deal?
  - ✓ What discounts or gross margin levels do you expect to have to sell at?
  - ✓ When is the deal forecasted to close?
  - ✓ Who needs to approve this deal?
  - ✓ What is the "get well" plan so you don't have to sell the future business at these same aggressive discount/gross margin levels?
  - ✓ Are there likely to be any special Terms and Conditions your organization might not enjoy?
- In Module 2 and 3, you qualify the deal using the BANT methodology.
  - ✓ B = Budget
  - ✓ A = Authority
  - ✓ N = Need/Business Outcomes
  - ✓ T = Timing
- Use the Relationship Map so you don't miss any important stakeholders.

- Projects are likely to get approved when they:
  - ◊ Are strategically relevant
  - ◊ Are tactically urgent
  - ◊ Provide rapid time–to–value

Action Items

Download these assets from the free resource page at SalesLeadersOnly.com/bookassets

- Rapid Assessment Review "Cheat Sheet"
- Relationship Map

STEP 3

COACH YOUR TEAM

CHAPTER 4

HOW WILL YOU COACH YOUR TEAM TO COVER ALL THEIR BASES?

We're almost there. One more step to go. Chapter #1 covered the system's first step by developing an intentional and deliberate cadence to inspect the Top 10–20 big deals in your sales funnel this quarter and next.

In chapter #2, we walked through a high-level overview of the Big Deal Roadmap.

Chapter #3 covered the system's second step and showed you how to assess the quality of your "Must Win" sales campaigns early in the forecast process by organizing a Rapid Assessment Review. The review uses the BANT methodology to explore the Budget, Authority, Needs/Business Outcomes and Timing of your deal.

We also reviewed the Relationship Map to ensure you had a complete understanding of the key stakeholders and decision makers in the powerbase and an assessment of how they feel about your solution.

With these two steps completed, we're now ready to explore Step 3 of the system, which is coaching . And we'll use the Sales Strategy Review as our guide.

The Sales Strategy Review Includes the Broader Sales Team

For this meeting, I always include more members of the sales team. In addition to the sales leader and rep, I always include the technical presales resources assigned to the opportunity as well as other key resources if they exist. If the channel partner manager, alliance manager or professional services manager can add value to the campaign, I include them as well.

Once the Big Rock Review process gains momentum inside your organization, additional resources will want to attend the reviews to gain insight into your big deals. The challenge here is when people join the meeting, they feel compelled to add their opinion, and before you know it, the review gets sidetracked and takes way too long to complete.

Keep the meetings tight, and resist the urge to make the meeting a beauty contest where bystanders want to show you how smart they are.

In this step, you (as the sales leader) walk the team through the additional questions included in Modules 4 to 10 of the roadmap. Each question is intended to uncover additional information about the opportunity and challenge the team's knowledge of its campaign.

Here's Where the Sales Leader Is the Coach

As I mentioned earlier in the book, this second meeting is an excellent opportunity for you (as the sales leader) to coach the team through the campaign's steps to help ensure nothing gets missed.

It's essential that the team feels the meeting is a productive place to explore what they know and DON'T know about their deal.

When I run a Sales Strategy Review with a team that has never done one before, I always begin with my pilot example from chapter #1. I remind everyone that the review's goal is to help ensure the team leaves the meeting with a better sales strategy and execution plan than when we started.

If a pilot with 25 years of experience goes through a preflight routine or checklist, so should they!

As a leader, you're going to do 10–20 Big Rock Reviews every quarter and get very good at determining which teams are close to their deals and which teams aren't.

Salespeople are reluctant to share what they don't know if they FEAR being judged or criticized. Your role is to demonstrate and accept that "unsure" is a good answer to your questions. If the first thing you do is blame the team for not knowing something or missing a step, the meeting gets shut down pretty quickly.

Your goal for each review is to help coach your experienced teams by guiding them and your newer teams by teaching them the best practices they may not have yet discovered.

When Done Well, Sales Teams Will Want You to Review Their Deals

You'll know you're adding value to the team when sales reps volunteer to walk through their deals using the Big Rock Review process with you, even before adding their deal to your hit list.

It's a great feeling to have the team WANT your inspection and coaching on their deals!

Don't worry if you've been reviewing big deals in an ad-hoc way all these years, leveraging your instinct and experience. The Big Deal Roadmap will be your guide. You can fake it till you make it. It won't take long before you get very comfortable with the process and make it your own.

While I've done hundreds of reviews using these same questions, you may have more relevant questions to bake into your review process, based on what you're selling. Remember, the idea here is to create an intentional and deliberate process or system you can use in a repeatable way.

Change the questions if you have more insightful ones based on your industry. It will only make your review process even better!

Step 3 of the System— Sales Strategy Review

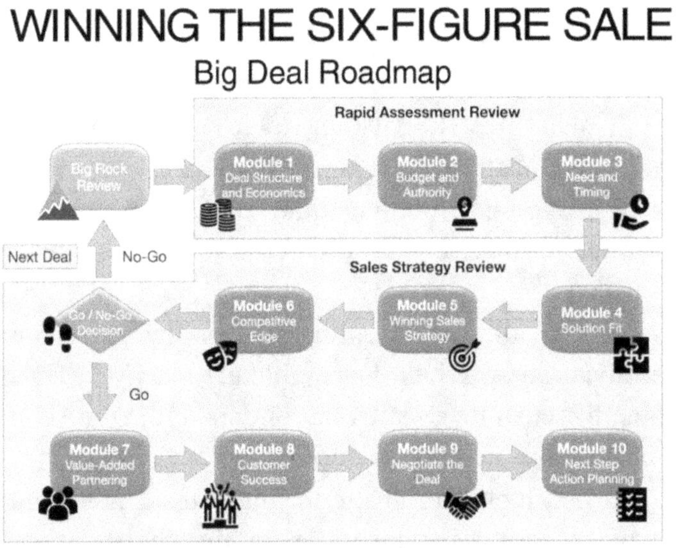

Diagram 8—Big Deal Roadmap

BEFORE each review, I get the rep to complete the Sales Strategy Review questions template and return their answers to me and the sales team at least 24 hours before the review.

In my half-day **Winning the Six-Figure Sale** course, I provide all the questions in a downloadable Microsoft® Word template, so the teams don't have to reinvent the wheel.

Let's work through many of the most useful questions I use so you have a good feel for what I cover in the Sales Strategy Review.

Module 4—Solution Fit

I start this module by asking the team:

- What are the customer's selection criteria, and are we a good fit?

Does the team understand the customer's requirements well enough to determine if our solution is a good fit?.

This is all part of ruthlessly qualifying from a technical perspective. We're unlikely to have everything the customer wants, but understanding if we're a 50% fit vs 80% fit, is essential.

I often look over at the technical team members to make sure I include them in the conversation. While the sales rep is the quarterback, it's always good to solicit feedback from other team members in the review who may have a different perspective.

Then I ask:

- How has the customer discovered our value?

PowerPoint presentations with deeply technical data and jargon may be necessary, but after the customer has sat through a few vendor presentations, they all start to sound the same since all vendors make the same claims.

You can help your customer discover your value through all sorts of activities, demos, proof of concepts, white papers, conferences, user group meetings, customer reference calls and HQ visits for executive briefings.

The list gets long.

If all the customer has done is heard your pitch and seen a short demo, you're in trouble. The next question is:

- What part of your value proposition has grabbed the most customer attention?

The rep must put herself in the customer's shoes. Understanding what's essential to the customer is all part of helping them discover value—from their perspective, not yours.

And the final question I often ask makes the sales leader a bit uncomfortable.

- Has the sales leader met the customer in person or on a Zoom video call?

This is a big deal for the team, and if the sales leader hasn't been involved enough to visit the customer, that's another red flag!

Module 5—Winning Sales Strategy

- What is your strategy to win, other than low price?

This is a big topic, and we spend a fair bit of time in the review discussing our approach to the deal.

- Is this an upgrade, tech refresh, rip and replace, land and expand, and/or new workload expansion?

Each one of these strategies will drive different sales activities and resources, so it's really important at the outset to get the entire team clear on the sales strategy and approach. The two key questions are:

- Who is the incumbent technology provider?
- Who is the primary competitor, and what is their strategy to beat you?

I'm always surprised when the sales team gets so focused in their own kitchen that they neglect to pay attention to the incumbent or the primary competitor. You can't lay traps and land mines if you don't know whom you want to blow up.

This last question in this module is specific to the tech industry. If you're selling hardware, software or networking equipment, you may not view cloud solutions as competitors.

Trust me, while you may not be considering the cloud an alternative, I guarantee your customer is.

Think about this next question and be prepared to answer it or suffer the consequences.

- What part of the customer's cloud strategy is competitive with the solution you are proposing?

Stop and review this last question again!

Amazon, Google, and Microsoft cloud offerings are grabbing huge chunks of the customer's IT budget. In addition to your direct competitor, make sure you consider how the cloud and these cloud hyperscalers might affect your deal.

Module 6—Competitive Edge

Early in the sales campaign, most teams try to figure out how to position their products as the best thing since sliced bread. That's not the kind of edge I'm referring to here.

Ask yourself this:

- How are you perceived in the account? Are you a product vendor, credible source, problem solver or trusted advisor?

Happy ears off. What would the customer say about your position in their account? How do they perceive you?

Here are a few more questions to determine your competitive position.

- Do you have access to power?
- Have you met the key decision maker(s) in person?
- Who is your coach, and are they sharing key inside information about how your campaign is being perceived inside the account?

Remember earlier in the book, I talked about a lesson from previous economic downturns where buying authority was being reduced, and approval to spend money was requiring more signatures from people higher up in the organization.

The question here is, "Do you have access to power, so you can ask the person who signs the check how they feel about your solution?" If you don't, can you partner with someone who does?

In my experience, you can win big deals without access to power. It's riskier, but it can be done.

I've rarely seen a team win a big complex deal without a coach, i.e., someone attending the meetings you'll never get invited to and sharing G2 (competitive intelligence) about how your campaign is being received.

The coach doesn't need to sell on your behalf. You want your coach to share what's going on inside the account so you can understand what part of your strategy is resonating with your prospect.

Developing a coach takes time, especially if it's for an account you've never sold to before. Get started developing a coach early in the campaign so you can gain their trust and help them be successful.

Go/No-Go Decisions Are Often Difficult

At this point in the review, I often pause and ask the team if they're ready to make a Go/No-Go decision.

Have we learned enough to validate that we have a good shot at winning the deal? Or are we best to bail now, before we waste any more cycles on a deal that's stacked against us?

Giving up on a deal, especially if the reps' pipelines are limited, is very difficult to do, but that's the whole point of the review—to never waste time or resources on big deals you can't win.

Here's an example: I was doing a Big Rock Review with a sales team in Ottawa.

As we worked through the deal, it was pretty clear the team was not selling very wide and deep and had not met many people inside the account.

The customer was in the public sector and was going through a formal RFP (request for proposal) process, so they weren't permitted to meet with vendors. We had a good sense of the technical specifications based on the RFP document. The rep believed we had an excellent opportunity to win based on our product's capabilities alone.

The rep was prepared to spend hours of her time and commit enormous resources from other team members to pursue the bid, even though some of the most basic non-product-oriented questions had not been answered during the Rapid Assessment Review.

So, I looked at the sales rep and said, "Based on what you know, what is your strategy to win, other than low price?"

Crickets (silence). I looked at her boss and said, "You know what we need to do."

The rep was really upset, but a big part of the value you get from a Sales Strategy Review is to objectively look at how wide and deep the account team is selling. Answering an RFP for a deal you have not been involved in has a 1 in 20 chance of success. So, we bailed on the deal.

As a side note, the technical resource, who was part of the deal review, took me aside after the meeting and thanked me.

He had been telling the rep all along that we had no chance of winning, but since the rep had no other significant deals in her pipeline, she wasn't prepared to stop. Left alone, she would have gone on fighting and wasted a lot of people's time that could have been better spent on other deals.

Ruthless qualification can be painful but is critically important to everyone on the team!

Module 7—Value-Added Partnering

When I ran NetApp Canada, we did about 75% of our business through Value-Added Resellers (or alternate pathways). At Veeam Software, the number was 100%.

The whole strategy behind selling with partners is about gaining leverage. Can you do more business and reach more customers by partnering with other organizations in the ecosystem?

For some sales teams, partnering can be very frustrating. Some reps are control freaks and need to do everything themselves.

I've often heard sales reps say, "The partner adds no value. They don't even know how to demonstrate or configure our equipment."

Think about this for a moment. Partners generally handle multiple product lines from many vendors. Rarely will a partner know more about your technology than you do.

Partner value comes in several flavors:

- They understand your technology better than you do (rare).
- They have sold to the account before and have access to power and are likely an approved vendor (valuable).
- They have previously established selling vehicles and can use them to reduce the time

and increase the probability of getting a purchase order when you forecast it (very valuable).

As I said, partners can add value in many ways beyond just understanding how your products work.

Figuring out how to leverage the partner's team to add value to the customer is the sales rep's job.

Here's a question I often ask to understand how well the rep is partnering:

- Have you and your partner rep shown up in front of the customer together?

If the answer is no, that's another big red flag.

Some sales reps are very reluctant to use partners and need to do all of the work themselves. They'll process the order through the partner at the very end of the campaign because they have to. This approach adds no value or leverage and frankly defeats the whole purpose of partnering in the first place.

It's not difficult to tell how the rep feels about partnering. If it's negative, you need to get to the root cause and address it asap before it sidetracks the whole deal.

Module 8—Customer Success

I love this section of the review. I can tell how much a rep cares about their customer by asking:

- What is your strategy to ensure customer success before you get your purchase order?

- What risks could cause the project to fail?
- What services are required to ensure success, and who will deliver them?

If a sales campaign takes months to close, it's usually because the solution is complex.

There is nothing worse than getting off to a poor start with a new customer because you didn't consider all the training and skills transfer required to ensure their success.

You have no chance of closing any additional business until the customer is satisfied with the initial sale.

If you stumble right out of the gate, you'll risk your ability to get the annuity follow-on business you were hoping for in the first place.

Customers don't care what you know unless they know that you care. The time to show them you're interested in their success is before you take their order!

Sell, Install, Support

Sell, install, support was a mantra I learned working at IBM years ago. Sales teams are well advised to write these three words down in a prominent place at their desks. Your customer's success depends on you executing across all three of these dimensions.

Module 9—Negotiating the Deal

If you've developed a great relationship with the customer and feel like they want you to win, what could go wrong?

This last set of questions often look way more straightforward than they are. I ask them to confirm if the sales team has done all their homework.

- What is the customer's approach to negotiating with vendors?
- How many rounds of negotiating with the customer do you expect?
- With whom will you be negotiating? The IT department, the end user, the procurement department, or all three?

Before you can develop your negotiating strategy, you need to understand the answers to these negotiating questions. There is no point giving the customer your firm and final offer if there are two more negotiating rounds yet to come.

What if you've never sold to this customer before? How will you know how close to the finish line you are?

In Module 6, we talked about the benefit of developing a coach. Here's a great example of how a coach can help.

Let Your Coach Be Your Guide

Your coach wants you to win; that's why we call them a coach. They will give you insight into how the final negotiating process will go from the customer's perspective. They may not tell you exactly what price you need to be at, but they will guide you through the process and help make sure you don't get blindsided at the last moment.

Without a coach, all you can do is ask the customer and hope for the best. Often the customer will cooperate, but sometimes they prefer to hold their cards close to their vest so as not to give up any leverage they may have in the negotiation process.

Module 10—Next Step Action Planning

From my perspective, the sales rep is the quarterback of the campaign. The rep doesn't have to do everything themselves but needs to ensure everything gets done.

Like the orchestra's conductor, they don't play all the instruments, but they are responsible for making sure the music sounds beautiful and flows seamlessly.

It's the sales rep's responsibility to track all the action items from both the Rapid Assessment and Sales Strategy Reviews and to publish meeting notes with action items after each meeting.

One Final Question—My Favorite!

The last question I use in the review is one of my favorites. I got this question from Ivan Brinjak, the vice president of sales at Long View Systems in Toronto. I liked it so much, I've used it ever since (with his permission, of course).

The Look Back Question:

- If the prospect were to notify you today that you lost the deal, what fatal flaws in your campaign do you think they discovered that led to the loss?

- How will you address the flaws now, before you get the bad news phone call?

This look back question forces the team to look at their campaign from the customer's perspective. I encourage the team to use this question early and often. Sales teams tend to drink their own Kool-Aid®, and this question forces them to take their happy ears off!

So, There You Have It

You've now completed all 3 steps in the 3-step system. So how do you take what you've learned and implement it in your business, given how busy you already are? That's a great question that we cover in the final section, The Path Forward.

Chapter Review

Here's a quick summary and action items to help make sure you caught everything we covered.

- Once you've determined the deal is well qualified, organize the Sales Strategy Review with the sales leader, rep and technical resources.

- Keep the meeting tight, and only include additional team members who can add value to the deal strategy and execution plan.

- Have the rep complete and return the review questions template at least 24 hours before the meeting so everyone can read and digest the answers.

- Make the review a positive, proactive coaching session, and don't shut down the conversation by criticizing the team for missing steps.

- Your goal for each review is to help coach your experienced teams by guiding them and your newer teams by teaching them the best practices they may not have yet discovered.

Here is a sample of questions to ask in each module of the review.

Module 4—Solution Fit

- What are the customer's selection criteria, and is your solution a good fit?
- How has the customer discovered your value?
- What part of the value proposition has grabbed the most customer attention?
- Has the sales leader met the customer in person?

Module 5—Winning Sales Strategy

- What is your strategy to win, other than low price?
- Is this an upgrade, tech refresh, rip and replace, land and expand, and/or a new workload expansion?
- Who is the incumbent technology provider?
- Who is the primary competitor, and what is their strategy to beat you?
- What part of the customer's cloud strategy is competitive with the solution you are recommending?

Module 6—Competitive Edge

How are you perceived in the account? Are you a product vendor, credible source, problem solver or trusted advisor?

- Do you have access to power?
- Have you met the key decision maker(s) in person?
- Who is your coach, and are they sharing key inside information about how your campaign is being perceived inside the account?

Module 7—Value-Added Partnering Comes in Several Flavors

- The partner understands your technology better than you do (rare).
- They have sold to the account before and have access to power (valuable).
- They have previously established selling vehicles and can use them to reduce the time and increase the probability of getting a purchase order when you forecast it (very valuable).
- Have the vendor and partner teams shown up in front of the customer together (priceless)?

Module 8—Customer Success

- What is your strategy to ensure customer success before you get your purchase order?
- What risks could cause the project to fail?
- What services are required to ensure success, and who will deliver them?
- Sell, install, support. Focus on all three dimensions to ensure customer success.

Module 9—Negotiating the Deal

- What is the customer's approach to negotiating with vendors?
- How many rounds of negotiating with the customer do you expect?
- Will the deal be negotiated with the IT department, the end user, the procurement department or all three?

Module 10—Next Step Action Planning

- The sales rep is like the conductor of the orchestra. She doesn't have to play every instrument but is responsible for the quality of the music.
- The rep is also responsible for publishing meeting notes and action items from the reviews to help keep everyone accountable for the next steps.

Use the Look Back Question Often Throughout the Review

- If the prospect were to notify you today that you lost the deal, what fatal flaws in your campaign do you think they discovered that led to the loss?
- How will you address the flaws now... before you get the bad news phone call?

Action Items

Download these assets from the free resource page at SalesLeadersOnly.com/bookassets

- Big Deal Roadmap

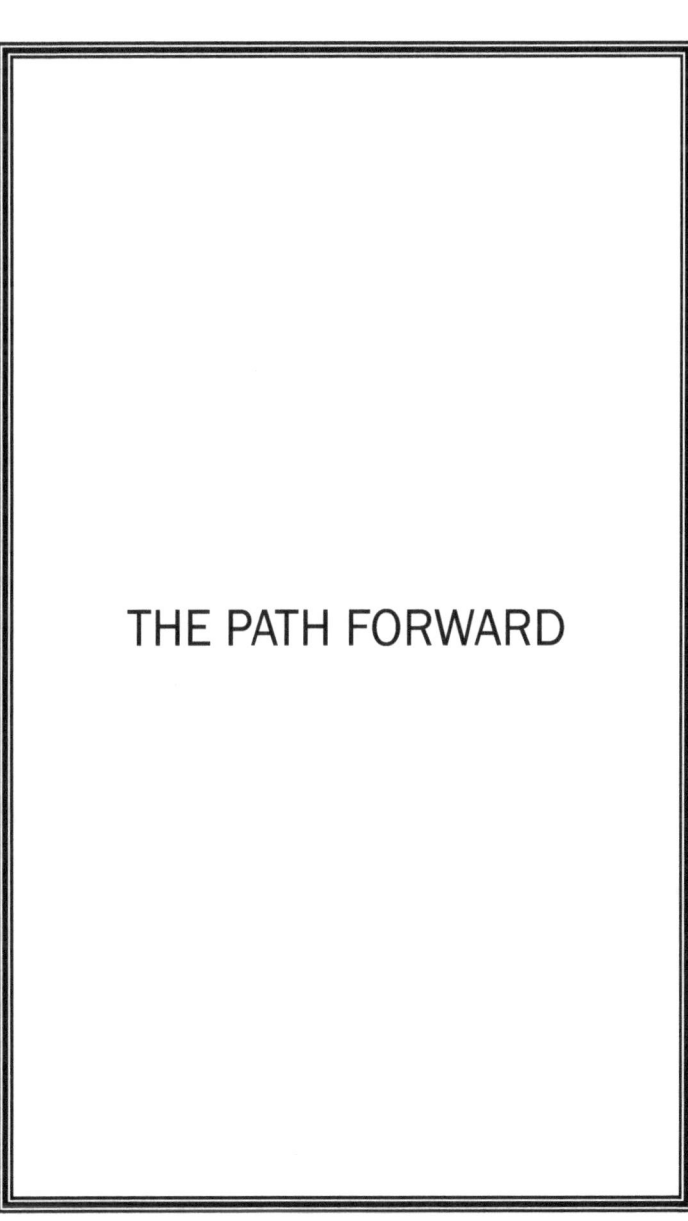

THE PATH FORWARD

CHAPTER 5

IMPLEMENTING THE 3-STEP SYSTEM IN YOUR BUSINESS

At this point, when I teach my program live, I often sense a growing level of frustration from the sales leaders in the class as they begin to think about how they would implement everything we've covered.

Step 1: Build a repeatable cadence to inspect the sales funnel and identify the Top 10–20 big deals this quarter and next.

Step 2: Complete a Rapid Assessment Review for each big deal to assess how well it's qualified.

Step 3: Once qualified, complete a Sales Strategy Review to coach the team through the big deal roadmap.

Inspect, assess, coach. It's not rocket science, so why do sales leaders begin to grow anxious right about now? Perhaps you're feeling the same way.

What's the Issue?

How difficult can it be to prioritize 10% of your time to focus on the big deals you know need more attention?

Let me ask you a few questions:

- Can you see how building a repeatable inspection cadence into your business might help to get more focus on your big deals?
- Do you think your team would benefit from a more consistent approach to assessing and qualifying their deals?
- Would your sales team appreciate another set of eyes on their deals to help coach them through the roadmap so they execute more successful sales campaigns?

Is your head nodding?

"Yes, Jeff, this all makes great sense, but who has the time to learn the system and then implement it? I'm already so slammed for time doing everything that's expected of me. I can't see the forest for the trees."

My day is already so busy:

- Recruiting, hiring, onboarding, and retaining an all-star sales team.

- Inspiring, empowering, coaching and motivating, while pairing business and revenue objectives with appropriate growth initiatives.

- Training new hires on the sales process, ensuring standards of success are clearly articulated.

- Consistently delivering revenue targets quarter over quarter and year over year.

- Accurately forecasting the business on a weekly, monthly and quarterly basis.

- Directing sales activities within my business, setting expectations, providing mentorship.

- Prioritizing the team's efforts, holding the team accountable for building their pipeline and executing each phase of the sales cycle.

- Coaching the sales team to uncover customer needs, develop champions, present specific use cases, demonstrate the differentiated value of our products and services.

- Negotiating favorable pricing and terms by selling value and return on investment.

- Working as a team for the most efficient use and deployment of resources; collaborating with sales engineering, channels/alliances, professional services, product, legal, marketing, and engineering teams to create a seamless customer experience.
- Using CRM systems extensively.

Wow, does this sound like a day in your life as a sales leader?

I took this list of activities right from a first-line sales leader's job description on LinkedIn. Amazing, isn't it? But that's what is expected of a sales leader, especially one on the front lines.

And while it's the life you've chosen, that doesn't make the job of getting everything done any easier.

No Simple Answer

Now, I wish I had a simple answer to where you find the time to implement a new approach to managing your big deals. I don't. But I do have a few ideas that have helped other sales leaders clarify where to begin and how to get started.

My first suggestion is to schedule some time with your boss and have a conversation.

If you go to her and say, "I'm so busy doing my day job, I can't see the forest for the trees. I want to implement a new system to manage my big deals, but

I don't know where to start! Can you show me where to begin??

My guess is that if you lay your problem at her feet, she'll tell you what she always tells you when you bring her problems without solutions, which is, "Figure it out; that's what I pay you for."

She probably won't use those words, but that's what she's thinking. Either way, that's not much help.

Instead, Here's What I Suggest

Build a list of all the things that take up your time. The LinkedIn job description will give you a pretty good place to start. Divide the list into two categories:

1. Critical few
2. Maintenance many

If you're not familiar with these terms, think about it this way. The *critical few* are 20% of your activities that account for 80% of your results. These are your high-impact activities.

The *maintenance many* are all those other things you do in the day that combine to give you 20% of your results. The maintenance many are often the place to look for time savings. Then take that list and do a start, stop, continue on it.

- What activities do you want to START that could make a big impact on your business that you aren't already doing? Add inspect, assess and coach!

- What activities can you STOP doing that would have little impact on your results? These activities take a critical eye to identify. Some of the things you spend time on made sense at one point but no longer give you the return they once did. Stop doing them, and take them off the list.

- What activities do you need to CONTINUE to do as part of your day-to-day responsibilities (the maintenance many)?

Once you've organized your start, stop, continue activities, take that same list and revisit the *critical few* and *maintenance many*. Does your list look different than when you began?

Now you're ready to take the list into your boss's office and have that conversation.

It Might Go Something Like This

"I've been thinking about how to carve out more time to focus on my big deals. Can I walk you through an exercise I've done to see what you think?"

"I'm looking for your feedback to see how I can re-prioritize my activities to carve out 10% of my time to focus on the critical role of inspecting, assessing and coaching my team's big deals."

Different conversation, right?

Now you're taking a proactive approach to your responsibilities and looking for feedback to see if you have any large gaps that your boss might be allergic to.

This is an excellent time to get agreement that there are some activities that you used to do that will be dropped from the list so you can get more focused on your big deals.

It's worth checking with your boss to make sure you're not planning to drop something that's important to them that might have some unintended consequences if you just stopped doing it.

Once you've completed this conversation with your boss, schedule time at your next sales meeting to walk your team through the same discussion. It's important they understand how you plan to re-prioritize your time to get laser-focused on their big deals.

This is also a great opportunity for you to introduce your new approach to helping your team WIN THEIR SIX-FIGURE SALES.

As I said earlier, there are no silver bullets here.

We all have the exact same 1,440 minutes each day. You can't change that, but you can control how you use those minutes to get the biggest bang for your buck.

If you're a do-it-yourselfer, you can take what you've learned in this book and begin implementing the 3-step system on your own. There is enough meat and downloadable assets here for you to get started and potentially be successful.

But building a new system to inspect, assess and coach your team through their "Must Win" sales campaigns is a lot like turning a large flywheel.

The first few turns can take a lot of effort, but once you get things rolling, the momentum you build will help transform the way you run your business.

Dedicating 10% of your time to implement my 3-step system will give you advantages you may not have thought possible, such as:

- Hitting your forecast in a much more consistent way because your team is winning more big deals.
- Having less drama in your business because your deals are better qualified with fewer last-minute forecast surprises.
- Seeing your team be way more productive because they no longer waste time and resources on big deals they can't win.

If you'd rather not build the entire system on your own, let's explore the options in chapter #6, The Next Step.

THE NEXT STEP

I hope this book has helped you think differently about what's possible. Instinct and experience have taken you a long way but building a structured preflight routine will make you even more successful.

From my perspective, you have three options in front of you right now.

1. You can do nothing. Gravity is the killer of good intentions. I see this all the time. Change is good, just not for me!

2. You can use what you've learned and do-it-yourself by building a system leveraging the tips, tools and strategies I've shared in this book.

3. You can prevent any false starts by reaching out to me and scheduling a Big Rock Review strategy call.

If you're serious about exploring how to implement a system of your own, you have nothing to lose.

There's no obligation, and scheduling is easy.

I understand that your goals are uniquely yours, which is why a conversation is the fastest way for us to determine if I can help.

If you're not quite ready to chat, you can visit my website at SalesLeadersOnly.com and visit my Leadership Training page or my Media page to learn more about my content.

You'll find several videos describing my programs. You'll even be able to watch several free one-hour masterclasses I've done with other organizations.

Some of my new customers start by having me complete a free one-hour masterclass for their leadership teams. The masterclass is an overview of what we covered in the book and is an excellent introduction to the concepts of inspect, assess and coach.

Almost 60% of the groups who attend a masterclass engage me to teach my half-day sales leadership course—**Winning the Six-Figure Sale**. Many also engage me to provide additional coaching to help implement the 3-step system in their organizations.

Maybe we're meant to work together. Maybe not. But like all good things, it all starts with a conversation where we can both ask questions and explore whether my program is a good fit for you right now.

I look forward to hearing from you, and more importantly, working together with your team(s) to help them win more *big deals*!

Great selling!

Jeff Goldstein

 Jeff@SalesLeadersOnly.com

 SalesLeadersOnly.com

 Linkedin.com/in/jeffgoldstein2

 416-723-1737

ABOUT JEFF GOLDSTEIN

Jeff is the founder of SalesLeadersOnly.com and the creator of the **Winning the Six-Figure Sale** leadership training program.

He helps sales leaders in technology win more big deals with his 3-step system. INSPECT, ASSESS and COACH, works. It is easy to understand and implement and can help sales teams close more big deals!

Over the last 20 years, Jeff has been building sales teams as VP, GM, and president of Canadian high-tech subsidiaries of large US-based tech companies, including HP®, Data General/EMC, NetApp and Veeam Software.

While Jeff is an engineer by training, he's spent his entire career grinding out a sales number every week, month, and quarter. He's always had income at risk and has been close to the field, close to customers, partners, and the sales teams who make it all happen.

Jeff has delivered his free one-hour masterclass and billable half-day training program to tech companies like NetApp, Veeam Software, Long View Systems, Ingram Micro®, FireEye®, Canadian Professional Sales Association and others.

Jeff loves spending time with sales leaders challenging them to think differently about how they run complex sales campaigns. As a business executive, author, consultant, sales trainer and coach, Jeff has helped transform how sales teams execute and win more big deals. The deals that move the forecast needle.

Jeff currently lives just outside Toronto, Canada, with his wife, Sandra. Their two kids have now left the nest, but the apple hasn't fallen far from the tree. Their son, Zach, is CTO of a software start-up, and their daughter, Virginia, is an outside sales rep working for Amazon Web Services. Jeff and Sandra have lived in seven Canadian cities, love to travel and see the world together.

To learn more about how Jeff might be able to add value to your next leadership meeting, quarterly business review or sales kickoff for either an in-person or virtual event, contact Jeff at:

Jeff@SalesLeadersOnly.com

You can also reach him on LinkedIn at:

Linkedin.com/in/jeffgoldstein2

He'd love to connect.

A SMALL FAVOR

Thank you for reading *Winning the Six-Figure Sale*. I'm positive if you follow what I've written, you will be on your way to transforming the way you inspect, assess and coach your team through the big deals that move the forecast needle.

I have a small favor to ask. Would you mind taking a minute or two and leave an honest review for this book on Amazon. Reviews are the BEST way to help others purchase this book, and I check all my reviews looking for helpful feedback. Visit:

SalesLeadersOnly.com/bookreview

If you have any questions or if you would like to tell me what you think about *Winning the Six-Figure Sale*, email me at Jeff@SalesLeadersOnly.com. I would love to hear from you!

Free Reader Resources!

Just to say thanks for reading my book, I've included downloadable training assets I developed as part of my 3-step system.

I refer to these resources throughout the book, and rather than reinvent the wheel, you can download and use them right away, at no cost whatsoever.

- ✓ Big Deal Roadmap: 10-step infographic of the "Must Win" sales campaign process.
- ✓ Big Deal Relationship Map: helps you keep track of where you stand with key stakeholders you need to meet and influence.
- ✓ The Rapid Assessment Review: a one-page "Cheat Sheet" with all the qualification questions.
- ✓ Top 10 Inspection Tracker: helps you keep score–Won/Lost/Deferred/No Decision.

DOWNLOAD HERE:

SalesLeadersOnly.com/bookassets